How To Love

MW01291619

<u>Love Yourself</u>

Stop Hurting, Stop Being Insecure, Gain Self Confidence, Begin Building Relationships, And Increase Personal Growth And Development Through Goals!

Mia Conrad

Copyright © 2014 Mia Conrad

STOP!!! Before you read any further....Would you like to know the Secrets of Transforming your life, overcome insecurities, develop leadership skills, and undeniable confidence in your personal, professional, and relationship life?

If your answer is yes, then you are not alone. Thousands of people are looking for the secret to have unstoppable confidence and self-driven power in all areas of their lives.

If you have been searching for these answers without much luck, you're in the right place!

Not only will you gain incredible insight in this book, but because I want to make sure to give you as much value as possible, right now for a limited time you can get full **100% FREE access to a VIP bonus EBook** entitled **LIMITLESS ENERGY!**

<u>**Just Go Here For Free Instant Access:**</u>

www.PotentialRise.com

Legal Notice

All rights reserved. Without limiting the rights under the copyright reserved above, no part of this publication may be reproduced, stored in or introduced into a retrieval system, or transmitted, in any form, or by any means (electronic, mechanical, photocopying, recording, or otherwise) without the prior written permission of the copyright owner and publisher of this book. This book is copyright protected. This is for your personal use only. You cannot amend, distribute, sell, use, quote or paraphrase any part or the content within this eBook without the consent of the author or copyright owner. Legal action will be pursued if this is breached.

Disclaimer Notice

Please note the information contained within this document is for educational and entertainment purposes only. Considerable energy and every attempt has been made to provide the most up to date, accurate, relative, reliable, and complete information, but the reader is strongly encouraged to seek professional advice prior to using any of this information contained in this book. The reader understands they are reading and using this information contained herein at their own risk, and in no way will the author, publisher, or any affiliates be held responsible for any damages whatsoever. No warranties of any kind are expressed or implied. Readers acknowledge that the author is not engaging in the rendering of legal, financial, medical, or any other professional advice. By reading this document, the reader agrees that under no circumstances is the author, publisher, or anyone else affiliated with the production, distribution, sale, or any other element of this book responsible for any losses, direct or indirect, which are incurred as a result of the use of information contained within this document, including, but not limited to, -errors, omissions, or inaccuracies. Because of the rate with which conditions change, the author and publisher reserve the right to alter and update the information contained herein on the new conditions whenever they see applicable.

Table Of Contents

Introduction

I want to thank you and congratulate you for purchasing the book, *Love Yourself: How To Love Yourself NOW! - Stop Hurting, Stop Being Insecure, Gain Self Confidence, Begin Building Relationships, And Increase Personal Growth And Development Through Goals!.*

This book contains proven steps and strategies on how to eliminate your insecurities and negative perceptions about yourself and build a more meaningful life.

It is often said that you cannot love another person unless you love yourself. This statement is often said in television shows and you often read this in books that it has become a cliché; but what does it really mean to love yourself? This book will help you understand the concept of self-love and will give you answers to the common questions about self-love. It also contains techniques that you can use to increase your self-esteem, self- confidence and self-love.

This book will help you appreciate yourself more and become your very own best friend. It will help you improve your sense of self-love and self-worth so you can attract healthier and more fulfilling relationships and live a life that is filled with happiness, acceptance and success.

Thanks again for purchasing this book, I hope you enjoy it!

Chapter 1 - Why Do Some People Love Themselves More Than Others?

Self –love is a popular buzz word nowadays. It has been widely used in many psychology books and it has been a hot topic on talk shows like Oprah. Many psychologists agree that self- love is necessary in achieving happiness and success in life. However, self-love is not something that we are born with. Self-love is heavily influenced by our social conditions, situation, perceptions, perception of other people and even our upbringing. This is the reason why some people love themselves more than others.

The term self-love was created by a well-renowned psychologist known as Erich Fromm. Erich Fromm proposed that loving oneself is different from narcissism or conceit. The intensity of one's love for himself is heavily influenced by the level of his sense of self-worth, self-confidence, self-respect and self-esteem. People who believe that they are valuable and worthy of love tend to love themselves more. People who have low self- worth, on the other hand, tend to neglect themselves because they do not believe that they are worthy of love and affection, not even from themselves. People who also have confidence in their own abilities and are secure of themselves love themselves more that those who have low self-esteem.

Aside from having a healthy self-esteem and self-worth, most people who love themselves grew up in a warm and supportive environment where self-love is heavily encouraged. People who develop healthy self-love in their adulthood often have very loving and encouraging parents. They are brought up in a nurturing and loving home where they were appreciated and accepted for who they are. People who love themselves are brought up in a home where it is alright to make mistakes and they are accepted for who they are. People who love themselves more are brought up in an environment that is secure and safe.

One of the reasons why some people love themselves more than the others is the difference in mental conditioning. There are those who are conditioned by their parents or authority figures that they are not worthy of love. Here are some of the reasons why some people have difficulty loving themselves:

1. They were overly criticized when they were young –People who have low self-esteem and who have difficulty loving themselves are often overly criticized by their parents or authority figures. They are often punished whenever they make even the slightest mistake. They are also often abused emotionally and physically. When a person is often abused and maltreated by people who are supposed to show them all the love and affection that they need, they would feel that they do not deserve to be loved. They will most likely have low self-esteem and will have difficulty showing love and kindness to themselves.

2. They were neglected when they were young – People who have difficulty loving themselves are often raised by parents who regularly neglect their needs. People who were left by their parents at a very young age spend their whole life wondering why they were left by their parents. It is difficult for them to love themselves because they do not know how it feels to be loved in the first place.

3. They lived in a loveless home – Some people are blessed to have loving parents, however, there are also children who are unfortunate to have parents who consistently fight with each other. When a person grew up in a home that's full of conflict, it is often difficult for them to love themselves.

4. They went through traumatic events – If a person was abused as a child or he is a victim of a heinous crime, it would be hard for him to like the world and himself. People who were victims of abuse often blame themselves.

5. Loving themselves is discouraged by their religion – Even in the 21st century, there are still religions that have a backward belief system. These religions teach people that it is wrong to love themselves. They were taught that it is selfish to love themselves. Because of this, some people

become codependent, regularly putting other people's needs above theirs.

6. Media project certain qualities as "lovable" – The media have a huge effect on people's self- esteem and sense of self-worth. Because of the media, people feel that if they do not look in a certain way or act in a certain way, they are not worthy of love and respect.

The voices and perceptions of the people we love and respect matter to us. When you grow up being heavily criticized by the very people that are important to you, you often sharpen your inner critic and routinely criticize yourself as well. Our ability to love and respect ourselves are heavily influenced by our self-worth and self-esteem. People who are insecure with themselves find self love a bit challenging. However, people who were raised in a very secure and loving environment find it really easy to love, respect and show kindness to themselves. In fact, self-love is part of their nature.

Chapter 2 - What Does It Really Mean To Love Yourself?

The concept of self-love was first introduced by a famous German psychologist named Erich Fromm in his 1956 book, The Art of Loving. According to Fromm, self-love is different from narcissism, arrogance, egocentrism or conceit. Generally, there are four components and elements of love – respect, care, responsibility and knowledge. Loving oneself, therefore, means respecting oneself, caring about oneself, knowing oneself intimately, accepting oneself and taking responsibility for oneself. Fromm first popularized the statement "In order to love another person, you have to love yourself first".

Self-love is easy for some people and a bit difficult for other people because of their upbringing and cultural influences. So what does self-love really look like?

When you love yourself, you are kind to yourself. You do not beat yourself too much if you make a mistake. When you love yourself, you are quick to forgive for all the horrible things that you might have done in the past. When you love yourself, you avoid working too hard to the point of exhaustion. You honor your body and its limits. When you love yourself, you eat healthy foods because you know that your body needs proper nutrition to function correctly and optimally.

When you love yourself, you do not neglect it. Do you regularly take vitamins to boost your immune system? Do you drink medicines when you need to? Do you regularly go to the salon for a manicure or a trim? Do you regularly exercise to make sure that you are fit and healthy? Loving yourself means taking care of your appearance and your body. It means making sure that you look your best most of the time. It means that you attend to your emotional, physical and spiritual needs.

When you love yourself, you accept yourself completely. When you love yourself, you like yourself a lot. You are comfortable with who you are. You like the way you look and you like the way you behave. When you love yourself, you do not say unkind words to yourself. You do not beat yourself up or call yourself "fat" and "ugly". Many psychologists say that our minds and body are somewhat connected so when you say positive things and have positive thoughts about your body, it will actually thrive.

When you love yourself, you do not say unkind words to yourself such as "You are stupid" or "You will never do anything right". When you love yourself, you make it a habit to affirm and regularly say kind words to yourself. Loving yourself means you do not berate or belittle your ability. You have faith in yourself and in your capabilities. You appreciate yourself and you treat it like your very own best friend.

Loving yourself also means you have healthy boundaries. You do not take advantage of others and you do not let others take advantage of you. You do not take any form of abuse or maltreatment from others. You draw a line of what you can do for others and what you can't. You will start building relationships that are founded on mutual trust, respect and support.

When you love yourself, you take care of yourself and your life in general. You make sure that your house is comfortable and clean. You have good hygiene. You wear comfortable, clean and decent clothes. You do your best in everything that you do. You take your responsibilities at work and at home seriously and you live a life that is grounded in your values, principles, and integrity.

Self-love means that you can cut yourself some slack every now and then. You give yourself treats every now and then and you always remember to have fun and just enjoy each moment. When you truly love yourself, it is easier for you to attract healthy relationships and love other people, too.

Chapter 3 - How To Develop Inner Peace Using Mindfulness Meditation?

Overworking or indulging yourself in many stressful situations and circumstances is a sign of lack of self-love. If you truly love yourself and you are being kind to yourself, you will take time to slow down and relax. If you truly love yourself, you'll make an effort to quiet your mind, silence your inner critic and control your thoughts.

Mindfulness meditation is a technique that is used by many spiritual mystics to train their brain, relax their mind and their body and achieve inner calm and inner peace.

If you do not love yourself, your mind is filled with critical and negative thoughts. You constantly berate and dislike yourself and you think harsh thoughts. Mindfulness meditation can help silence your inner critic and promote peace. When you regularly practice mindfulness meditation, you are less judgmental of yourself. You will get to know yourself a little bit more and accept yourself for all that you are. Mindfulness meditation can help you attain inner peace because it helps you take care of your feelings, your body and your perceptions. It develops self-awareness and as discussed earlier, self-awareness is a very important component of self-love.

Here's how you can practice mindfulness meditation to increase your love for yourself:

1. Choose a place in your room or in your office where you can meditate and where you will not be disturbed or distracted.

2. Sit in a comfortable chair and gently close your eyes. Notice everything you feel, smell, taste or hear.

3. Take deep breaths, inhale through your nose and exhale through your mouth, allowing your rib cage to expand.

4. Focus on your breath. In your mind, say "Inhaling" and then, "Exhaling".

5. Once a thought comes up, label it as "Thinking". Do not judge yourself or your thoughts, just bring back your focus and your thoughts to your breathing.

6. Stay focused in the moment, do not think about your past or worry about your future.

7. Breathe and let go of all the negative labels that you regularly give to yourself. Let go of all the negative thoughts that you have about other people. Let go of all your negative perceptions about the world and about yourself. Just let everything go.

8. Say a little prayer of gratitude and slowly open your eyes.

To reap the benefits of meditation, you have to practice it regularly. It also helps if you practice mindfulness throughout the day – while you are working, eating, or walking. As you eat, involve all of your senses. Pay attention to every bite, pay attention as you chew. As you walk from the parking lot to your office, pay attention to every step. Pay attention to the surroundings. Be aware of what your body does and consumes and the thoughts that come into your mind.

When you are aware of all your negative thoughts and feelings and you decide to let go of them without judging yourself, you are more in control of your life and you attain inner peace. Inner peace is the best gift that you can give to yourself.

Chapter 4 - The Importance Of A Morning Routine And Self Love

Most people tinker their laptops and check their Facebook account first thing in the morning. They spend the first 20 minutes of their day browsing and checking other people's relationships, vacations, work, wardrobes, and family through social networking sites. This ritual may appear harmless at first, however, sociologists repeatedly stress that social networking sites can wound people's self-esteem.

One disadvantage of social networking sites is that these sites encourage people to project an exaggerated version of their lives. People often boast and project happiness and perfect relationships in social networking sites when, in fact, they are also struggling to make ends meet. If you spend a lot of time on Facebook or other networking sites, you will tend to be discontented with yourself and your life. You would feel jealous of how other people lived their lives. You would end up comparing yourself and your life to other people's lives. This is dangerous because it brings feelings of low self-worth, discontentment and unhappiness.

If you want to increase your love for yourself, you have to create a morning routine that will increase your self-confidence, your self-worth, your self-esteem, your self-love, and will empower you to give your best in everything that you do, every day.

Here's a morning ritual that you can do every day that will help you start your day right and increase your self-love:

- Wake up earlier than what is required. It is important to get up right away when you wake up in the morning. You will feel tired and irritated if you keep on pressing the snooze button on your alarm clock. As soon as the alarm goes off, get up right away.

- Instead of reaching for a cigarette right after waking up, reach for a glass of water. Hydrating yourself right after you wake up will help you become more energized and healthy. It is also a great way to start your day.

- Take time to stretch. Stretching will help you condition your body for a busy day ahead. It will also help you connect with every nerve and every cell in your body.

- Think of the things that you are grateful for. Take time to appreciate all your blessings. Take time to be grateful for the little things that you often take for granted. Take time to be grateful for your car, your house, your family, your business, and your job. Be grateful for the people around you, your hard-working colleagues, and your kind neighbors.

- Visualize and think of your dreams. Loving yourself means allowing yourself to have dreams and ambition. Take time each day to sit down and visualize the future that you want. Think about the things that you want - big house, luxury car, successful career, or successful business.

- This is one of the most important step in your daily morning routine, take a time to look at the mirror and say kind things to yourself. Notice the things that you like about yourself. Notice your luscious hair, your fair and flawless skin, your beautiful eyes, or even your beautiful mind. Appreciate your appearance and accept your flaws. Refrain from judging yourself. This is not narcissism, but this is self-acceptance and self-love.

- Start your day right by having the right kind of breakfast. If you are used to eating the typical Western breakfast that consist of white bread, eggs, bacon, and ham, it is time to eat more fruits and vegetables. Instead of eating the typical Western breakfast, have a smoothie, vegetable soup, or fresh fruits. Eating a healthy breakfast is one of the best ways to love yourself.

It is important to start your day right, you will become more energetic and productive and as a result, you will be less stressed and anxious. If you have a positive and healthy morning ritual, your day will run smoothly.

Chapter 5 - Why You Have To Have Self-Discipline To Increase Your Self-Esteem And Love Yourself?

Self-discipline is defined as "the ability to control one's emotions and feelings and the ability to pursue something important despite of the many temptations to abandon it". It is the ability to manage your behaviors, moods and thoughts.

When you have self-discipline and self-control, you stand by your principles and you are in control of your life. Responsibility and integrity is a very important component of self-esteem and self-love. If you routinely abandon tasks and responsibilities and go against your values, you will eventually develop anger and disappointment with yourself. If you regularly pick pleasurable activities over the important tasks, your life will be a mess and it will be hard for you to achieve the things that you have dreamed of. Having self-discipline and self-control will enable you to sort out your life.

If you constantly say "no" to things that are not important or that are bad for you such as too much alcohol, junk food, cigarettes, watching too much TV and spending too much, you exhibit responsibility over your life and that is a sign that you love yourself. When you constantly say "no" to actions that are opposed to your inner values such as promiscuity, drug abuse, unethical work practice, and mediocrity, it is easier for you to be proud of yourself, and it is easier for you to love yourself.

If you constantly practice self-discipline and self-control, your life will be on the right track. If you regularly say "no" to junk food and other unhealthy food, you will be fit and healthy and it is easier for you to love your body. If you push yourself to get up every morning to jog and exercise, you are keeping your body in good shape. If you constantly pick studying over partying, you will later on get a good job and have a successful career. It is easier for you to love and like yourself if you have a successful career and a balanced life. If you spend hours and hours learning a skill, you will later on reap the rewards and use that skill to have a better life.

Self-discipline is a very important element of self-love and self-esteem. If you have self- discipline, you become more confident with yourself and your abilities. If you have self-discipline, you create a life that you want and deserve. If you have self-discipline, you feel in control of yourself and your life. Control over yourself and your life is the ultimate foundation of self-esteem and self-esteem is the ultimate foundation of self-love.

Chapter 6 - How To Stop Insecurity For Good And Regain The Control Of Your Emotions?

One of the ways to show self-love is to eliminate and control all your insecurities and feelings of inadequacy. Many experts say that self-love, self-esteem, and self-confidence are based on an emotion. Self-confidence and self-esteem are built on how we feel about ourselves. If you want to build self-esteem and self-confidence and increase your self-love, you have to change how you feel about yourself.

To change your emotions and how you feel about yourself, you need to change your core beliefs about yourself and your self-image. If you have low self-esteem and you do not love yourself or care for yourself, chances are, you have a negative self-image. One of the most basic core of low self-esteem and lack of self-love is the feeling that you are not good enough. It is the feeling of inadequacy. That feeling may be associated with how you look or how smart you are or the amount of wealth that you have. The second core belief that needs to be changed is our belief or perception of how success should be.

If you grew up in a home that is filled with rules and "should be", you will eventually believe that you are not good enough unless you are "perfect". This is the reason why people who have low self esteem are often perfectionists. To eliminate your insecurities, you have to be realistic about your perception of success and acceptable behavior. To eliminate your insecurities and feel good about yourself, you have to be proud of your achievements.

You may not be a CEO of a multi-national company, but you are good at your middle management job, you have a car, you have a house, you have a lovely family, and you can afford to go on vacation to an exotic island as often as twice a year. You need to cut yourself some slack and thank the heavens for your blessings. You may not be as intelligent as Bill Gates and you may not be able to solve a complicated math problem, but you have enough intelligence to make good decisions and do your job well and you can also paint, play the guitar, or dance. To eliminate your insecurities, you need to appreciate your talents and gifts.

How you feel about yourself is just a result of the negative core beliefs that you have developed over the years. Once you adopt a positive self-image and adopt positive core beliefs about yourself, your self-esteem and self-confidence will skyrocket and you will love yourself more.

Chapter 7 - The Health Of Relationships In Your Life And How They Impact Your Love For Yourself

Our relationships have a great impact on our lives and they definitely have a great impact on the level of the love and care that we give to ourselves. Erich Fromm believes that a healthy self-love is the foundation of all the good and healthy relationships. You cannot love another person if you do not love yourself first.

If you do not love yourself, you will have poor boundaries and if you have poor boundaries, you would just let the people in your life walk over you. If you do not love yourself, you rely on other people or outside circumstances to feel better about yourself. If you do not love yourself, you tend to accept poor treatment from your spouse, parents, or friends because you do not feel that you deserve a better treatment.

However, as much as the love for yourself has an impact on the health of your relationships, the health of your relationships also has an impact on your love for yourself. If you have a spouse who regularly abuse you physically and psychologically, your sense of self-worth will eventually diminish and you will be conditioned to think that you deserve the abuse and that you do not deserve love.

If people that you care about regularly belittle you, you will have less confidence in yourself. When you are in a relationship with someone who constantly rejects you, you will eventually think that you deserve that kind of treatment. Unhealthy relationships are bad for you. Here are the signs that you are in bad relationships:

1. Your partner says bad and unkind words to you often. Your partner, parents, or friends overly criticize you.
2. Your partner or family members take you for granted and neglects you often.

3. You cannot thrive while you are in the relationship. Your relationship does not allow you to grow personally and professionally.
4. You feel that all your positive energies are sucked from you.
5. You keep on fighting and there's always conflict.
6. The other person has so much power and control over you. You do not feel that you are in control of yourself anymore.
7. You feel bad about yourself.

If you are in a bad relationship, you have to know if it can be saved or changed. If not, it would be best for your self-esteem to just leave. Leaving a bad relationship is one of the most powerful ways to show kindness and love to yourself.

Chapter 8 - The Importance Of Goals Regarding Self-Love And Confidence

If you have goals and you work hard to achieve your goals, you increase your chances of succeeding in life. When you frequently experience success in your undertakings, your self-confidence will increase and you will like and love yourself more.

Goal setting is one of the most powerful ways to improve self-love and build your confidence in yourself. Although self-love and self-confidence are deeply based on perception, you must not discount the fact that achievement and success have the power to skyrocket your confidence and your self-love. Having goals and aspirations in life will instantly boost your self-esteem and self-confidence.

But what is a goal? Most people say that they have goals in life. They always say that their goal is to have a Jaguar, a 10-bedroom house, and tons of money in their bank account. However, according to life coaches, these are not goals, these are fantasies and wishes that are common to most human beings. A goal is something that is carefully crafted and it changes and evolves as time goes by.

A goal is simply defined as a systematic envision or a desired result that a person commits to achieve. A goal is not much of a wish, but it is something similar with aim and purpose. When you have a goal, you have a strong sense of purpose and a strong sense of purpose is one of the most powerful sources of self-confidence and self-love.

Chapter 9 - 20 Tips For Setting The Perfect Goals

As discussed earlier, goals are not mere wishes. They are systematic and they give us a strong sense of purpose and direction. It is important to have goals in life; but in order to live a successful and fulfilling life, it is also important to have the right set of goals.

Here are some of the tips that are needed in setting the perfect goals:

1. Create goals that will make you happy – We grow up thinking that there is a certain template of what our goals should be. When we were young, we were conditioned to want more money, a big house, diamonds, and a luxury car; but is that what you really want? Do you think that it will make you happy? Scientists and psychologists say that happiness precedes success. People who are happy with themselves and with what they do for a living are often successful not only in their careers but in life.

2. Create Intrinsic Goals - As discussed earlier, we often fall into the trap of thinking that we should be successful in accordance with the society's view of what success is. Society wants us to chase money, beauty, wealth and fame. Intrinsic goals are the goals that would make us happy. Intrinsic goals help us grow as individuals. Intrinsic goals help you pursue personal growth or make a lasting contribution to the society.

3. Create Goals that Are Congruent to Your Principles – Take time to find out the things that are really important to you. Make sure that your goals are not in conflict with your principles and the things that you believe in.

4. Take a look at your life – Before you set a goal, you have to look at your life. What do you think is lacking? What are the parts of your life that you want to be changed or improved?

5. Set a deadline – A goal without a deadline is just plain weak. Setting a deadline will motivate you to increase your effort to achieve the goal.

6. Realistic – You need to set a goal that is realistic and achievable. This is not to say that you should not aim high. A goal of earning 1 million dollars within a year or even in 2 years can be reasonable, but earning 1 million dollars in a month is just unrealistic especially if you have not earned anything near a million dollars before.

7. Create positive goals – Structure your goals in positive statements. Instead of "Do not be late", go for "Be punctual". Positive statements are more empowering.

8. Identify your priorities – When you are setting a goal, you have to determine what your priorities are. Your goals should be aligned with your priorities.

9. The goal should be specific – Your goal has to be detailed. You have to specify when and where it should happen. You should be specific about what you want to accomplish. A goal that says "I want to be rich" is often not effective. You have to be specific about how much you want, when you want to get it, and what are the ways that you will use to get it.

10. The goal has to be measurable – You should be able to measure your goals because this will motivate you to exert much effort to achieve it. When your goals are measurable, you will know if you are making a progress.

11. Pick a model or inspiration – If you want to achieve something like build your own business or be successful in your career, carefully study those who have already achieved it. What were their goals and how did they achieve those goals?

12. Once you have achieved a goal easily, pick a more challenging and exciting goal – Your goals should be challenging and exciting. Some people pick goals that they

can easily achieve. If you pick a more challenging goal, you will feel more fulfilled once you achieved it.

13. Write down your goals – Your goals do not have enough force unless you write them down on a piece of paper. When you write down your goals, they become tangible and you become more motivated to work hard to achieve your dreams.

14. Visualize – Take time to think about your goals and imagine how it feels like to achieve your goals. Think about your life two to five years from now. Do you see yourself achieving your goals? How does it feel to live your dream life? How does it feel to be successful? You can also create a vision board where you can post the images that represent your goals and your dream life.

15. Break down your goals – If you have big goals, it helps if you break down that one big goal into several goals. This way, your goal is easier to achieve and you get to celebrate small successes and movements towards your bigger goals.

16. Brainstorm – Although goals should be personal, it is best to brainstorm with people who can help you create great goals. You can brainstorm with your partner, friends, sister, or a life coach.

17. Make your goal public – Once you have identified your goals, you have to make your goals public. This is a very effective goal-setting technique for many people. Broadcasting your goals can make you more determined to achieve them.

18. Create a detailed strategic plan – Don't just merely create goals, you have to create a detailed strategic plan on how you can achieve it. When you have a detailed plan, it is easier for you to achieve your goals.

19. Pick a goal buddy – Pick a goal buddy that will help you review your goals and track your progress. Your goal buddy will be the one to support you and cheer you on as you work hard to achieve your dreams.

20. Commit to your goals – Once you have set your goals, you have to fully commit yourself towards achieving it.

Goals are important and while the end in setting a goal is to achieve it, you will be rewarded by lessons, learnings and skill developments during the process. If you have a goal, your life will have a clear direction. You take the driver's seat of your life and you are in control of your life.

Chapter 10 - How To Measure Your Progress And Reward Yourself Each Day For Falling In Love With Yourself And Building Confidence

To effectively increase your love for yourself, you have to track your progress regularly. Here's how you could track your progress:

1. List the tasks that you need to do to exhibit and practice self-love. The checklist looks something like this:

   - Break up with my abusive boyfriend or girlfriend.
   - Say kind words to myself.
   - Look in the mirror each morning and appreciate my beautiful features.
   - Appreciate the blessings that I have received.
   - Set goals.
   - Follow through with my goals.
   - Visualize and affirm daily.
   - Exercise at least thirty minutes daily.
   - Eat more fruits and vegetables.
   - Travel to places I have never been.
   - Stand up against bullies.
   - Dress to kill.
   - Get a weekly manicure.

2. Write each task in a calendar. Print a calendar for each task. Every day, mark the date if you are able to do the task. This will help you track your progress and consistency.
3. Notice the changes in your relationships. If you practice self-love often, people will respect you more.
4. Notice the changes in your career. If you love yourself more, your career will thrive and you will become more successful in your line of work.
5. Create a monthly or weekly personal review. This is much like the quarterly review that you get at work. Take time to

review your progress and assess which strategies are working and which strategies are not working.

If you have already progressed and your love for yourself have improved, reward yourself by doing more loving things for yourself. You can go to a spa, eat the best ice cream in town, or eat out in a pricey restaurant. You can also buy yourself new clothes and new shoes. And lastly, give yourself a pat in the back. You deserve it!

Conclusion

Thank you again for purchasing this book on loving and taking care of yourself!

I am extremely excited to pass this information along to you, and I am so happy that you now have read and can hopefully implement these strategies going forward.

I hope this book was able to help you understand what self love really means and how to increase your self love.

The next step is to get started using this information and to hopefully live a more fulfilling and happy life!

Please don't be someone who just reads this information and doesn't apply it, the strategies in this book will only benefit you if you use them!

If you know of anyone else that could benefit from the information presented here, please inform them about this book.

Finally, if you enjoyed this book and feel it has added value to your life in any way, please take the time to share your thoughts and post a review on Amazon. It'd be greatly appreciated!

Thank you and good luck!

Preview Of:

The Ultimate Mindfulness Meditation Guide!

<u>Mindfulness</u>

Live In The Present Moment, Tame Your Mind, Get Stress Relief, And Understand Emotions And Feeling Good!

Introduction

I want to thank you and congratulate you for purchasing the book, "Mindfulness: The Ultimate Mindfulness Meditation Guide! - Live In The Present Moment, Tame Your Mind, Get Stress Relief, And Understand Emotions And Feeling Good ".

Mindfulness Techniques For Living In The Moment And Feeling Good!

This "Mindfulness" book contains proven steps and strategies on how to begin living life to the fullest when you live life in the present moment!

Our brains are very powerful tools, but the only problem is that if you don't know how to manage your brain it can sometimes take on a mind of its own - literally! This makes it very important that we understand how to observe and manage the thoughts, feelings, and emotions that naturally come in and out of our minds on a day to day basis.

In this easy to read and understand book on mindfulness you will easily come to understand how simple it is to begin living in the present moment with a little practice. And I am very confident this will be one of the best decisions you make of your life!

This book contains useful information regarding mindfulness meditation, breathing for mindfulness, and journaling to understand your thoughts and emotions better. You should use this book if you need guidance when it comes to practicing mindfulness and applying it certain aspects of your life, particularly your emotions. It also includes tips on how you can practice mindfulness better.

Thanks again for purchasing this book. I hope you enjoy it!

Chapter 1: What Is Mindfulness And How Can You Benefit From It?

The human mind gets distracted easily. It habitually examines past events and tries to anticipate future ones. You may think that being aware of your feelings, sensations, and thoughts is not a good idea. However, doing that in a way that suspend self-criticism and judgment may have a good impact on your life.

Mindfulness is basically the practice of becoming completely aware of the present instead of dwelling on the past or venturing into the future. It is a way of clearly seeing and paying attention to what is happening around you. While it cannot get rid of the pressure you experience, it can help you respond to it in a better and calmer manner.

Mindfulness can help you recognize and stay away from unconscious physiological and emotional reactions to daily events. It can provide you with a scientific approach to cultivating insight, understanding, and clarity. When you practice mindfulness, you will be able to be completely present in your life, and even improve its quality.

Mindfulness involves an increased awareness of sensory stimuli, so you really notice the sensations in your body and your breathing. You can achieve mindfulness through meditation, although you can also practice it through your daily living by focusing on the current situation and quieting your inner thoughts.

Mindfulness is actually a simple form of meditation. It is about observation with the absence of criticism and being compassionate with yourself. It lets you focus on your breathing as it flows throughout your body. When you focus on every breath, you are able to observe the thoughts in your head.

You are able to realize that these thoughts come and go, and that you are not really your thoughts. You are able to come to an understanding that feelings and thoughts are transient. You actually have the ability to choose whether or not you will act on these feelings and thoughts.

What Mindfulness Entails, Who Is It For, and How Is It Practiced?

Jon Kabat-Zinn states that mindfulness is about paying attention in a certain way without judgment, with a purpose, and in the present moment. Those who practice it learn how to pay attention on purpose by practicing especially created mindfulness meditation practices and mindful movements.

The practitioners can learn how to stop or slow down thoughts and reactions with adequate practice. This will allow them to experience the present moment as it is. Everyone has a tendency to harbor uninvited thoughts into their heads no matter how much they practice mindfulness.

This is alright, though. It is not really what your brain does that matters, but rather how you respond to its thoughts. If you begin to think about your thoughts or get frustrated with yourself for not being able to stay focused, you will lose your attention from the present moment.

On the other hand, if you acknowledge your thoughts and let them go without judgment, you will be able to retain your focus on staying in the present moment. Just like new skills, the more you practice this, the easier it will be for you to do it over and over. Basically, the more you practice mindfulness, the more you develop neuro-pathways in your brain and the easier it will be for you to stay in the present moment.

When you learn to experience the present moment, you are able to move away from unconscious and habitual physiological and emotional reactions to daily events as well as view things as they really are. You are also able to respond to these things wisely instead of being on auto pilot.

Mindfulness is for people of all ages, gender, or status. It is not a religion, so it does not really matter what your religious component is. Anyone can have the benefits of mindfulness, regardless of their belief system. Mindfulness actually has powerful medicinal benefits.

The most researched and recognized modern forms of mindfulness are MBCT and MBSR. These programs are typically taught for eight weeks, and the participants are asked to meet for two to three hours per week. There are also home practices in between the meetings.

The participants are taught numerous meditation practices that have already been proven to help lessen brain chatter as well as respond more easily to feelings and thoughts. Most MBCT and MBSR trainings include body scan exercises, walking meditation, sitting meditation, body awareness exercises, gentle stretching, and mindfulness meditation.

The Benefits of Mindfulness

According to research, mindfulness has plenty of benefits. For instance, mindfulness-based stress reduction (MBSR) and mindfulness-based cognitive therapy (MBCT) have found to be helpful with anxiety disorders, including generalized anxiety disorder, depression, relationships, sleeping, eating disorders, and stress management.

Anxiety disorders, such as generalized anxiety disorder or GAD may be reduced with mindfulness-based intervention. With the use of such method, patients with anxiety disorders can efficiently lessen their depressive and anxiety symptoms.

Likewise, patients suffering from depression can benefit from mindfulness-based interventions. Those with residual depressive symptoms and depressive episodes can reduce their ruminations and symptoms. Better results can be seen after a month.

According to a certain study, people with greater mindfulness tend to have better and more satisfying relationships as well as able to deal more constructively with stress. According to another study, people who practice mindfulness have less stress when faced with conflicting situations. They are also able to communicate better. Both of these studies have linked mindfulness with better relationships.

With regard to sleeping and eating disorders, mindfulness have also been found to be beneficial. Cancer patients, for instance, were able to reduce their sleep disturbance while improving the quality of their sleep.

Similarly, people with eating disorders are able to improve their condition. A group of women with bulimia nervosa underwent a mindfulness-based treatment program for eight weeks, and they were able to report significant improvements in their behaviors and emotions. They were also able to have greater compassion, self-awareness, and acceptance.

Furthermore, mindfulness can help people deal with stress better. Studies have found that mindfulness can help with daily stresses and more serious stresses, including life-threatening illnesses that are related to stress.

According to studies, mindfulness is beneficial in stopping ruminations over the things that result in stress. It basically helps people avoid harboring negative thoughts, as well as being anxious towards the future. It provides a break from stressful thought activities and even allows you to gain perspective.

Over time, mindfulness can cause long-term mood changes. Scientific studies show that mindfulness can prevent depression, and positively affect brain patterns associated with stress, anxiety, irritability, and depression. Other studies have also shown that people who regularly meditate require medical attention less frequently.

In addition, they become more creative, their memory improves, and their responses become faster. They are able to achieve resilience at home and work, as well as balance. Also, they are able to view situations more clearly. They recognize, stop, or slow down habitual and automatic reactions.

Myths with Regard to Mindfulness

Unfortunately, some people still have wrong notions regarding mindfulness. These people need to be educated properly regarding mindfulness-based interventions, so they can live more efficiently and happily.

Some people think that meditation is a religion. Well, this is not true because mindfulness is just mental training. Although a lot of those who practice meditation are religious, mindfulness is still not a religion. In fact, there are a lot of agnostics and atheists who also practice mindfulness.

Another false notion with regard to mindfulness is that mediators' need to sit cross-legged on the floor. Well, mediators' usually sit cross-legged, but this is not a requirement. You can actually sit on a chair if you do not feel comfortable sitting on the ground. You can even practice mindfulness while on a bus, train, or basically anywhere.

You do not have to spend an entire day practicing mindfulness. A lot of people refuse to practice mindfulness because they think that they are too busy. What they do not realize is that mindfulness does not require a lot of time. It can actually liberate you from the pressures of time, so you will have more of it.

There is nothing complicated about meditation. It is not even about failure or success. Even if it seems difficult, it will teach you valuable things regarding how your mind works. Hence, it will benefit you psychologically. Meditation will not prevent you from achieving important lifestyle or career goals.

Do not worry because it will not trick you into adopting a Pollyanna behavior towards life. It is not about accepting what is unacceptable. Meditation is about viewing the world with great clarity so you can make wise decisions. It will help you make the appropriate action with regard to things that you have to change.

Meditation can help you become more compassionate and more aware of your goals and values. It has also been clinically proven to be effective in fighting against stress, anxiety, depression, and exhaustion. It even works for people who are not depressed but are struggling to keep up with the high demands of society.

Thanks for Previewing My Exciting Book Entitled:

"Mindfulness: Live In The Present Moment, Tame Your Mind, Get Stress Relief, And Understand Emotions And Feeling Good!"

To purchase this book, simply go to the Amazon Kindle store and simply search:

"MINDFULNESS"

Then just scroll down until you see my book. You will know it is mine because you will see my name "Mia Conrad" underneath the title.

Alternatively, you can visit my author page on Amazon to see this book and other work I have done. Thanks so much, and please don't forget your free bonuses

DON'T LEAVE YET! - CHECK OUT YOUR FREE BONUSES BELOW!

Free Bonus Offer: Get Free Access To The PotentialRise.com VIP Newsletter!

Once you enter your email address you will immediately get free access to this awesome newsletter!

But wait, right now if you join now for free you will also get free access to the "LIMITLESS ENERGY" free EBook!

To claim both your FREE VIP NEWSLETTER MEMBERSHIP and your FREE BONUS Ebook on LIMITLESS ENERGY!

Just Go To:

www.PotentialRise.com

Made in the USA
Monee, IL
01 September 2020

40319581R10024